INFORMATION EXPLORER

SUPER SMART INFORMATION STRATEGIES

PODCASTING 101

by Kristin Fontichiaro

CHERRY LAKE PUBLISHING • ANN ARBOR, MICHIGAN

CHERRY LAKE Publishing

A NOTE TO PARENTS AND TEACHERS: Please remind your children how to stay safe online before they do the activities in this book.

A NOTE TO KIDS: Always remember your safety comes first!

Published in the United States of America
by Cherry Lake Publishing
Ann Arbor, Michigan
www.cherrylakepublishing.com

Content Adviser: Gail Dickinson, PhD,
Associate Professor, Old Dominion University,
Norfolk, Virginia

Book design and illustration: The Design Lab

Photo credits: Cover and page 17, photos courtesy of Kristin Fontichiaro; page 4, ©Leah-Anne Thompson/Shutterstock, Inc.; page 10, ©iStockphoto.com/ alubalish; page 19, ©JinYoung Lee/Shutterstock, Inc.; page 20, ©iStockphoto. com/BenDower; page 22, ©Vasaleks/Shutterstock, Inc.; page 23, ©iStockphoto. com/bonniej; page 26, ©Julián Rovagnati/Shutterstock, Inc.

Library of Congress Cataloging-in-Publication Data
Fontichiaro, Kristin.
    Super smart information strategies. Podcasting 101/by Kristin
Fontichiaro.
        p. cm.—(Information explorer)
    Includes bibliographical references and index.
    ISBN-13: 978-1-60279-953-0 (lib. bdg.)
    ISBN-10: 1-60279-953-9 (lib. bdg.)
    1. Webcasting—Juvenile literature. 2. Podcasting—Juvenile literature.
I. Title. II. Title: Podcasting 101. III. Series.
    TK5105.887.F65 2010
    006.7—dc22   2010004533

Cherry Lake Publishing would like to acknowledge the work
of The Partnership for 21st Century Skills. Please visit
www.21stcenturyskills.org for more information.

Printed in the United States of America
Corporate Graphics Inc.
July 2010
CLFA07

Table of Contents

CHAPTER ONE
What Is Podcasting?

What kind of radio show would you like to broadcast?

Have you ever listened to the radio and wished you had your own show? Do you like asking people questions? Are you creative? Do you enjoy acting things out? If so, podcasting may be the activity for you!

Podcasting involves the process of recording an audio or video file to share with others. Video podcasts are sometimes called "vodcasts." These files can be shared over the Internet and downloaded to computers. The files can also be loaded onto devices called media players. Say you record voices using computer equipment and add sound effects or music. The final product is called an audio podcast.

You can upload, or transfer, your podcast online. Be sure to ask a parent or teacher for permission and help first. Then you can share the podcast with friends and family. You can listen to your podcast on a computer. You can also make a CD with your project on it. Another option is to load it onto an MP3 player. In this book, we'll focus on creating audio podcasts.

You and your friends will be able to listen to the podcast that you create on your MP3 player.

TRY THIS!

There are hundreds of ideas that your podcast can explore. You could:

- make a commercial
- discuss your favorite book
- promote your favorite musicians or sports teams
- ask trivia questions
- give a play-by-play of a sports event
- do a weather report
- interview friends, older relatives, or experts
- create a radio play
- pretend you're a journalist from the past reporting on a historical event

With few exceptions, if you can think it up, it can be a podcast! Try coming up with three ideas for podcasts that aren't on this list. If you have a hard time thinking of ideas on your own, ask two or three friends to brainstorm with you.

What should you have to get started? To make a podcast, you will need

- a computer with an Internet connection;
- software for making a podcast—one option is the free software Audacity (turn to the Find Out More section of this book for the URL);
- a headset with a microphone attached; you could also use a microphone on a stand that connects to your computer through a USB connection;
- a site or medium to which you can upload your podcast, with an adult's permission.

Sometimes, it's fun to make podcasts with a partner. Interviews and radio plays are two examples of group podcasts. To make either of these, you'll need to use a microphone on a stand. You could also connect two headsets together using a special splitter called a Y-connector.

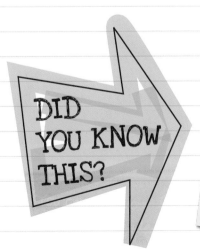

DID YOU KNOW THIS?

Don't worry if you don't have this podcasting equipment. Check with your school or public library. Teachers or library media specialists may have supplies that you can borrow. They may even be able to help you make the recordings.

CHAPTER TWO
Planning Your Podcast

Quick! Stand up and start giving a tour of the room you are in right now. How did it go? Did it take you a while to figure out what you wanted to say and the order in which you wanted to say it? Were there things you left out? Did you give the tour in the best order? Would you have done a better job if you were given a chance to plan out your thoughts first? Probably!

Great information explorers know that planning is a very important part of making a podcast. A good podcasting project to start with is a commercial. Commercials are short. They're usually not longer than 30 seconds. You can plan and make them quickly.

Thirty seconds isn't very long. You need to know what you are going to say in order to use the time effectively.

TRY THIS!

When you listen to the radio, which commercials are the ones that you enjoy the most? Which do you remember? Turn on a radio. Listen to some of the ads. On another sheet of paper, list the features that grab your attention. Those are the things that you'll want to include in your commercial to make it exciting, too. Listen for:

- music
- sound effects
- voices
- word choice
- humor
- emotion

How do these features improve a commercial? Do they make you want to know more about the product or service being offered? Think of the main message of a commercial as a pizza. Music and other features are a bit like the toppings that take a plain pizza to the next level.

Can you think of a song that might help sell pizza?

9

Speaking of pizza, let's say we're going to make a commercial podcast advertising your parents' amazing homemade version. Being a good information explorer means staying organized. For a commercial, you will want to organize your ideas like the experts. Listen to a few more radio commercials. Many of them

- **start with a hook.** When people listen to the radio, they aren't always carefully listening to the commercials. A hook is often an exciting

Think about what makes pizza so tasty. That information will help you create a good commercial.

opening phrase or sentence that grabs the listener's attention. "I bet you're hungry right now," is one example. "Imagine a pizza with plenty of fresh tomato sauce and gooey cheese," is another option. Some commercials feature a short song called a jingle to introduce a product or service.

- **offer reasons why people would enjoy the product or service.** For a pizza commercial, you might talk about the great toppings or crust.

- **end with a memorable sentence.** A pair of closing sentences could be, "Does your mouth water at the thought of a crispy crust and plenty of cheese? Then you can't miss my mom and dad's homemade pizza!" Some ads conclude by repeating the jingle or introducing a new part of the jingle.

Following this pattern is a good way to start. You will soon become more comfortable with podcasting. Then you can use whatever formula works best for you.

Some podcasters prefer to make outlines. They write out the hook and list a few important words or points. Then they write out the final sentence. An outline for a pizza ad could look something like this:

Index cards are a great way to organize your ideas.

I. HOOK: Imagine a pizza with plenty of fresh tomato sauce and gooey cheese.

II. IMPORTANT WORDS OR POINTS

   A. Pineapple

   B. Green pepper

   C. Sausage

   D. Crust

   E. Fresh out of the oven

III. CLOSING SENTENCES: Does your mouth water at the thought of a crispy crust and plenty of cheese? Then you can't miss my mom and dad's homemade pizza!

What happens when it is time to record? You turn the items on the list into full sentences and practice repeating them.

Some podcasters prefer to write out every word of their speech or script. They type up the script in a big font. The text should also be double spaced. This helps make it easier to read. A pizza ad script might look something like this:

Your script should be exciting and is easy to read.

Mmmm . . . Imagine a pizza with plenty of fresh tomato sauce and gooey cheese. Picture it covered with your favorite toppings: sweet pineapple, spicy sausage, and green pepper. And the crust? Perfectly crisp! You won't be able to wait to get to that part! Nothing tastes quite like my parents' pizza, fresh out of the oven. Does your mouth water at the thought of a crispy crust and plenty of cheese? Then you can't miss my mom and dad's homemade pizza!

Now practice saying those words until you feel comfortable. Then record your voice.

Draw your ideas out on paper.

Mouthwatering!

Do you organize your thoughts better using images instead of words? Try a storyboard. Draw a picture that stands for each sentence in your commercial. Use these images as an outline for your ad.

TRY THIS!

It's time to start planning a radio-style commercial. How about advertising your favorite food? The goal is to plan a commercial that will make your friends want to buy or eat what you suggest. Use an outline, storyboard, or full script to organize your thoughts. No matter which format you choose, remember to include a hook and reasons why your food is delicious. Don't forget to also include a memorable ending. Don't want to make a commercial about food? You can also create one for:

- your favorite book
- your favorite sports team
- an upcoming school event

continued ——→

You could also plan a special kind of commercial called a public service announcement (PSA). PSAs suggest that listeners take an action that will benefit their lives or the lives of others. You could create a PSA that discusses the importance of:

- buckling seat belts
- returning library books on time
- following school or bus rules
- recycling
- attending a community event

You may be eager to start creating your podcast, but don't rush through this planning stage. Careful thought and organization will set you up for success at all steps of the podcast-making process.

CHAPTER THREE
Recording Your Podcast

Now that you have planned your podcast, you are ready to start recording.

You've planned your podcast. Now rehearse what you will say. Review your outline, script, or storyboard. Practice your lines from beginning to end. Do you feel confident that you've gotten the words down?

Next comes the exciting part: recording your podcast! First, you'll need to plug your microphone into your computer. Your computer may also have a built-in microphone. Open the recording software program you've chosen. Depending on its age and model, your computer may already contain software for recording audio. Ask an adult to help you look if you're not sure. If not, ask an adult for permission and help with downloading recording software. Remember, one option is Audacity.

Most podcasting software programs have a button to start recording and another to stop recording. There is also a button that allows you to go back to the beginning of the recording, and another to play it. Take a minute to find those buttons on your computer screen.

Now you want to prepare your environment for recording. Make sure you are recording in a quiet space. If you are wearing jingly jewelry, take it off. If a fan, furnace, or air conditioner is running, is it very loud?

When you are ready to record, you should set your papers down in front of you. If you hold them in your hand, the microphone might pick up a rustling sound.

Make sure you are comfortable so you don't have to move around a lot while you record.

TRY THIS!

The time has come to make your recording. Get set up in a quiet place. Set your script, outline, or storyboard down. Take some deep breaths. Ready? Set? Record!

Directions for specific software will vary. The process will likely follow some version of the following:

- Press the Record button.
- Recite your lines, referring to your notes if necessary. Be sure to speak clearly.
- When you're done, press Stop.
- Press the button that allows you to backtrack to the beginning of your recording.
- Press Play to hear your audio clip.

When recording, remember you can always push Pause or Rewind.

What do you think? If you are happy with the result, save it according to the software's directions. If not, delete it and try again.

A podcast featuring your voice is great. But one with music or sound effects could be even better.

Music can help you set a mood. The next time you watch a TV show or a movie, listen carefully. Notice how music can communicate information about the setting or emotions of the story. How could the tempo or instruments of a piece of music give your podcast a relaxed, exciting, or serious tone?

Choose any music or sound effects for your podcast carefully. Many times, less is more. You want any added sounds to compliment your message, not overshadow it.

If you play an instrument, think about writing some music for your podcast.

Sound effects help listeners imagine events that they can't see. There are many sound effects that you can add to your podcast. The sound of an oven timer dinging can help the listener realize that something is cooking. The sound of an owl hooting can hint that it is nighttime. What could the sound of a barking dog or screeching car brakes add to a podcast?

You can make your own music and sound effects. Simply bring your instrument to the microphone and play away! Think creatively about how to make sound effects, too. Say you wanted to create footsteps. You could put shoes on your hands and "walk" on the table-top near the microphone to imitate footsteps.

You may wish to use music from a CD. Hold on! You need permission from the people who have created the music or sound effects before you can use them. For this reason, it is better to use audio you make yourself. You could also use music or sounds from a Web site that gives you permission up front. When in doubt, ask an adult to make sure you have permission to use any music or sound effects. You may also have to give credit to the audio source.

TRY THIS!

Do you enjoy radio or TV ads about movies? Those ads are called trailers. They are designed to make the listener or viewer want to see the movie.

Imagine a movie or TV show that you saw recently. What kind of trailer could you make to promote it? Using the same format choices for planning a commercial, organize what you will say. Then record your trailer. Following your software's directions, add music or sounds. Will the music play the entire time you are talking? Will it play only at the beginning or end, or at an especially exciting point? When you are done, save your project.

What kind of podcast can you make to advertise your favorite movie?

CHAPTER FOUR
Editing, Revising, and Exporting

Have you ever written an essay for school? Your teacher may have asked you to edit or revise your work before creating a final draft. You should do the same with podcasts. When you create a podcast, you want to make sure it's your best work. Only then should you share it with others. Editing and revising

⌐ Editing is one of the most important parts of creating a good podcast.

involve reviewing what you have created. For your podcast, this includes your words, the music, and any sounds. The idea is to make thoughtful changes until the final product is just the way you want it. Here are some questions to ask yourself as you edit and revise:

- **Is it easy to hear my voice?** If not, moving the microphone closer to your mouth can help. So will speaking more loudly. Some podcasting software lets you adjust the volume of your voice, music, or sounds. You want to balance the sounds. That way, nothing drowns out the other parts.

You can ask your friends to listen to your podcast and give you their ideas for making it better.

- **Do I have dead air?** Dead air is any period of silence during a broadcast. When you podcast, there may be dead air at the beginning of the recording or after you finish speaking. Dead air could also occur at any point you may have paused to collect your thoughts. You can take out those empty spots and sound like an expert!

- **Am I saying what I want to say?** You may not realize that it would be better to say something in a different way until after you've recorded yourself. It's always fine to go back and record your words again.

Taking the time to edit and revise your podcasts says much about you as an information explorer. It shows you care about your work and your audience. You want your listeners to hear only your best efforts.

Don't be nervous when recording your podcast. You can always revise it.

TRY THIS!

So far, you have created two projects: a commercial and a trailer. Go back and listen to what you have recorded. Listen for places where you could adjust the volume. Could you add or change the music and sounds? Is it a good idea to tweak your words? Take some time to edit and revise your work. When everything sounds just the way you want it, export the files following your software's instructions. As always, ask an adult for help if you need it.

Revise and edit your podcasts until you think they are perfect. Then, save, export, and publish them.

Are you finished editing and revising? If so, you're ready to publish your podcast in an Internet-friendly format. Software companies usually call this exporting your file. You will save your file as a one-word file name (with no spaces). The software will add a code such as .*mp3* or .*mp4* to the end of the file name.

CHAPTER FIVE
Publishing Your Podcast

You're near the end of the podcasting process. But there are still a few more steps to go. Remember, podcasts are meant to be shared. You can have an audience of one listener or an audience of thousands. It's time to publish your podcasts. Here are some options:

- E-mail them to friends or family members.
- Post them to a wiki or Web page.
- Burn them onto a CD.
- Load them onto an MP3 player.

MP3 files are just one way to share podcasts with your family and friends.

One of the most important things to remember about publishing podcasts is to stay safe online.

Online Safety Checklist

1. Ask a parent, teacher, or librarian for permission before you publish anything.
2. Check your work before you publish. This time, you are checking for any personal details about yourself. You want to keep that information out of your podcasts. This includes your last name, address, school, or teacher's name. You want to protect your privacy.
3. Think about who you want to hear your podcasts. Choose a publishing format that fits your needs from the list on the previous page.

Remember to keep other people's feelings in mind when you create and publish a podcast. Never use a podcast to spread rumors about or speak poorly of others.

TRY THIS!

Podcasts can be a creative option for a school project. Imagine that your teacher has asked you to report on a famous person by researching his or her biography. You could choose a famous historical person or someone living today. Albert Einstein and Michelle Obama are two options.

With a partner, research the person's life. Then work together to create an interview. One of you will play the famous person. The other will be the interviewer. Create an outline or write a script of your interview in advance. "Where did you grow up?" and "Why are you famous?" are some questions you could include. Use your research to give factually accurate answers. Practice what each of you will say. Then record a podcast of the interview. Consider adding theme music.

Research the famous person's life and create an outline.

UNITED STATES HISTORY

Research:

With your partner, edit and revise the interview. It should flow smoothly and naturally. Then publish your podcast. Ask a teacher or librarian for help if you need it.

When you are finished, try repeating the process. This time, you and your partner should switch roles. If you were the interviewer, for example, you should be a different famous person.

Do you see how a podcast can put a special spin on a school assignment?

Practice with your partner before you record.

Podcasts are a fun and exciting way to share information. So get creative and get going. The podcasting possibilities are endless!

Glossary

biography (bye-OG-ruh-fee) writings that explain a person's life story

MP3 (em-pee-THREE) a format for storing audio data or a computer file in such a format

podcasting (POD-kass-teeng) the process of making podcasts, or audio or video files that can be downloaded to a computer or media device

public service announcement (PUHB-lik SUR-viss uh-NOUNSS-muhnt) a commercial that encourages people to take a specific action or think a certain way, often to improve their lives or the lives of others

sound effects (SOUND uh-FEKTSS) noises added to a podcast to help actions come to life or seem more realistic

storyboard (STOR-ee-bord) a series of sketches or pictures that outline the events that will happen in a story

tempo (TEM-poh) the speed of a piece of music

upload (UHP-lohd) transfer a file from a computer to another device

USB (yoo-ess-BEE) a special type of connection for attaching specific devices to computers

wiki (WI-kee) a Web site that allows users to add and edit content and information

Find Out More

BOOKS

Jakubiak, David J. *A Smart Kid's Guide to Internet Privacy*.
New York: Powerkids Press, 2010.

Sawyer, Sarah. *Career Building Through Podcasting*. New York:
Rosen Publishing, 2008.

Sturm, Jeanne. *MP3 Players*. Vero Beach, FL: Rourke
Publishing, 2009.

WEB SITES

Audacity

audacity.sourceforge.net

Ask an adult for permission and help with downloading this
free recording and editing software. You'll also find instructions for downloading the free LAME converter. It is needed for
exporting your podcasts in MP3 format for publishing.

BBC—Podcasts: World News For Children

www.bbc.co.uk/podcasts/series/wnc/

Check out some short news podcasts from the British
Broadcasting Corporation.

KidsHealth—Safe Cyberspace Surfing

kidshealth.org/kid/watch/house/internet_safety.html

Read helpful tips for staying safe online.

Index

About the Author

Kristin Fontichiaro is a clinical assistant professor at the University of Michigan and a former school librarian. She loves libraries, research, and making podcasts! This is her second book for kids.